Acknowledgments

I owe so much to a close network of friends and associates for their help and support in getting this project completed.

First, thank you to Brian Forbes and Catherine Tsai; two very talented writers who provided their editing expertise and unfiltered feedback.

Thanks to John Jenson for his spot-check on authenticity and to Mark Kimbrel, a graphic designer who applied his gifts of layout and illustration to add life to this book. Finally, to my friend Keith Marcks, I so appreciate you sharing your fire of all things print and publishing.

I also want to express my gratitude to those countless friends (you know who you are) who encouraged me to put on paper these concepts that have been such a passionate part of my professional life.

Thank you to my daughters, Leigh and Kelly, whose professional careers are a reflection of much of what is discussed in this book. I am extraordinarily proud of you both. And to my remarkable wife, Betsy, who believed all along. You are an inspiration to me and to others in ways you will never know or fully appreciate. This time and this place, was designed for you my dear.

D1564982

The Job of Getting a Job

I am haunted by a contemporary American failure. That is, the gap between your desire to secure your first meaningful job after college, and the absence of the functional knowledge needed to accomplish that.

Understand this; it's not solely your fault. With diploma firmly in hand, you're bright, eager and ready to embark on a professional journey that should offer you opportunities to grow and contribute in ways you could never imagine.

You may have worked with a career counselor at college prior to graduation. You probably even attended a few job fairs. You got advice from your parents. And you spent $100 on a service that helped you prepare your resume. You're on LinkedIn. You are scouting job openings on line every day. You're smart.

So what's wrong? Why haven't you landed that great position? I believe a big slice of the blame can be placed squarely on the doorstep of your institution of higher education. Quite simply, they failed to adequately prepare you for professional work. They never taught you about the *job of getting a job*.

Now, you obviously learned several important things in college. The simple fact that you've earned a degree shows employers you care enough about your professional development to invest the necessary time and energy. Don't underestimate that. It counts.

But where I believe most schools fall short is in teaching you the soft skills that are absolutely essential in winning your first quality job. By this, I mean the ability to network properly with the right professionals, generate interest, create opportunities, sell yourself and close the deal.

The good news is these are skills that can be practiced consistently and acquired quickly. Better yet, if you follow the suggestions offered in this guide, you will distinguish yourself among the vast pool of other college graduates seeking the same opportunities you are. Differentiation is essential.

Why should you listen to me?

Who am I to instruct you on all the finer points of winning your first great job? I certainly don't have any special training in human resources or advanced degrees in talent management. In fact, I'm a fairly average middle-aged professional who would be difficult to spot in a crowd. But what I do have that should be of infinite value to you is *understanding*. By that, I mean a keen understanding of what hiring managers and companies look for in a young professional and an understanding of the character qualities that must be packaged and presented effectively to win the best positions.

How did I acquire all this magical insight? I got it the long way. Through trial and error, missteps and successes over a 35-year career of hiring and managing hundreds of individuals, I've simply learned what organizations want and need in associates. I recognize the qualities all great associates possess. And I can teach you what those things are.

As the son of Depression-era parents, I certainly inherited a perspective that work is a gift to be treasured, and meaningful work that advances your career has to be earned. There are no shortcuts in the *job of getting a job*, at least not for winning the quality positions.

The real world

*"But here in the real world, it's not that easy at all
'Cause when hearts get broken, it's real tears that fall"*
- Alan Jackson, Here in the Real World

I will help you win your first meaningful job. That is no small promise. Simply finding a quality position is challenging, let alone finding one that will become a launch rocket for your career.

But know this, there are great positions to be had. Companies, large and small, are looking for talented professionals capable of adding immediate value, helping them compete and grow. Winning those jobs, however, will prove to be elusive, and yes, as Alan Jackson laments, even heartbreaking for most job seekers. Why? It's because this is a contact sport that takes effort, and few candidates actually understand the amount of hard work required.

If you will apply yourself and be the exception, then your chances of success increase exponentially. There is one caveat, however. You must execute on all of the actions identified in this book and you must do so with conviction and consistency. These are essential practices that will set you apart and help you win your first meaningful job.

Hard truths

- True networking is a hand-to-hand endeavor and has little to do with being on line socially.

- Hiring managers don't care about the school you attended or your GPA; just that you graduated.

- Hiring managers also understand you know very little about business; so don't act like you do.

- The majority of interviews are blown in the first two minutes and most candidates never know why.

Where the jobs are

You may be a talented pre-med scholar hoping for a residency at Johns Hopkins Hospital, or a recent MBA graduate looking to work for a large consulting firm, or a programmer seeking technology opportunities with Apple or Google. Great. Pursue your dream.

Don't forget, however, that small businesses – generally considered those companies with fewer than 500 employees – are a driving economic force of American enterprise. The numbers don't lie. Small businesses employ over half of the private sector workforce. This is important, because small businesses are often looking for individuals with broad and more general capabilities.

I won't pretend to know where the best jobs are. I will tell you, however, that the best fishing involves uncovering those rarely publicized opportunities, and those often occur within smaller organizations. This guide is designed to help you identify not only your natural gifts that should be of interest to all organizations, but also those broader character qualities that are specifically of interest to smaller firms.

Let's get started. Your career is waiting.

Chapter 1
Know Thyself

"If you can't tell a compelling story in 60 seconds about why you're uniquely qualified to be hired, then you have little chance of being remembered."

When I graduated from the University of Arkansas in 1980, I had no idea what profession I would pursue. I'd played four years of collegiate golf for the Razorbacks but recognized that an extended career on the PGA Tour was a dream not supported by my talent.

In addition to not knowing what I wanted to do, I didn't understand what I was equipped to do. This made my first efforts at networking and interviewing painful and ineffective. Don't make this same mistake.

Your gifts
I believe every individual is uniquely designed with special gifts. Given the right work environment, these innate gifts afford you the ability to thrive professionally while also contributing to the

success of the company that has chosen to employ you. The challenge is in knowing what these gifts are and knowing how to package them in a natural conversation where employers can readily see the value you offer.

This requires you to conduct a personal inventory or assessment of yourself. Here are a few easy steps to help you identify these personal qualities and to prepare yourself to discuss them.

Craft your personal story

1. Begin by listing what you believe are a few of your natural gifts – things you truly enjoy and are proficient at (don't concentrate too much on your areas of academic study; this can be misleading).

2. Next, ask your family members or close friends what they think your gifts are (you may be surprised what you hear).

3. Evaluate all the qualities you've listed and refine the list to just 3-4 areas you're convinced represent your best natural talents.

4. Now, write a few sentences which capture the gifts you've highlighted; this will become the framework for your 60-second elevator pitch of your personal story.

5. Finally, practice your story (yes, many, many times and in front of a mirror!), so you can deliver it well, comfortably and at a moment's notice.

When you begin your networking process, you'll likely modify your story slightly to best position yourself for a specific influencer or organization, but it's important to remember that your story always should be authentic, accurate and natural.

A story of my own

In retrospect, if I had conducted a personal inventory upon graduation, it would have looked like this:

I like writing – both fiction and non-fiction. I enjoy reading and have an inquisitive mind. I'm comfortable meeting new people and I make friends easily. I'm intrigued with graphic design, architecture and visual concepts that bring an element of order and structure.

Subsequently, when asked by a prospective employer why I should be considered, my story would have been:

- *I enjoy building new relationships and find it easy to do so.*

- *I have the ability to communicate well – both in writing and in discussion.*

- *I like research and am a quick learner.*

- *I can package difficult concepts in ways so others can more easily understand.*

If these are qualities that would be of value to your organization, then I believe I can be a strong contributor right away.

Notice anything? I just identified qualities – unique to me – that most employers hunger for when hiring new associates. I said **nothing** about acquired skills (of which I had very few upon graduation) and I said **everything** about the types of behavioral traits that companies desire.

This is all about the importance of packaging, which is the ability to position you in a succinct and compelling manner. It's about defining the elements you know are important to an employer and making sure they associate those things with you, and nobody else.

Remember, you are competing for a quality job. The hiring manager is likely interviewing several qualified candidates. You need to be memorable. Having your story buttoned up tight is vital to distinguishing yourself among others.

Chapter 2

A State of Mind

*"**Attitude** and **energy** are everything. Well . . . maybe not everything, but in combination, they'll win 98% of the time."*

A few quick words before we discuss the tactics of winning your first meaningful job. I believe there are three important parts of what I would consider having the right mental mindset. There are others, I'm sure, but if you focus on these, you'll not only have the fortitude to persevere in the job of getting a job, but you'll exhibit qualities that are highly valued by employers.

1. Go up tempo
You have to believe you'll be successful. I believe you will be! Empty your mind of those pervasive negative thoughts and view this process as a new exciting adventure. Because, the truth is, it will be an adventure. You'll meet interesting and influential people along the way. You'll discover new industries and positions you never knew existed. Your confidence and communication skills will grow. You'll become disciplined, focused and successful.

Certainly there will be moments when you are discouraged. That's normal. Disappointment is simply part of the journey. How you deal with that disappointment defines character and it becomes visible. This is important to remember: The good companies hire for character, and your character is always on display. A positive outlook simply keeps you motivated, moving and executing on the essential actions needed to win a great position.

2. Find your humble self
This is a personal bias of mine, but I look for the virtue of humility when I'm interviewing a candidate, and I believe many other hiring managers do as well. Humility doesn't mean you lack confidence (next mental element), but rather it is an indication that you are simply appreciative of being considered for the opportunity and you recognize you have much to learn.

Don't try to highlight what you know, because at this fledgling stage of your career, you don't know much. Focus instead on who you are. Candidates who try to impress with their intelligence or knowledge often find themselves the first discarded in the interviewing process.

3. Channel a quiet confidence
So how do you blend humility with confidence? It's easy. Exude confidence on the things you know are important to employers. You are a hard worker, coachable and collaborative. These things count and you wouldn't be where you are if you didn't posses these qualities.

Have confidence in your abilities to work well within teams, to learn new tasks and to apply more effort than others, so that you'll quickly make a positive impact. These are all powerful conversational elements in an interview, and great characteristics to have when you embark on your career.

It's who you are, not what you've done
Stellar resumes and private college diplomas aside, the hiring process always comes down to personal chemistry and the right fit.

People hire people they would like to work with. So be authentic and genuine. Positive attitude and energy are everything to an employer. Think of it this way; you are a malleable block of clay, ready and willing to be shaped into a true contributor. This is what employers are looking for. This is what they'll hire when they see it.

Chapter 3
Your Initial Network

"There is an art and a science to networking. Surprisingly, the science is relatively easy. Make no mistake, the art is where all the magic happens."

If you remember nothing else from the suggestions I offer in this guide, remember this: Your network is the single most important part of finding your first great job. Treat your network as a precious gift. Few things are of greater value professionally.

Start early
If possible, you should start building your first network a full semester before you expect to graduate. The competition for quality jobs is strong and will only intensify when large waves of candidates begin searching after graduation. Having established contacts already in place will only help you accelerate your opportunities once you have your diploma. So who should be included in your first network? It may surprise you.

Friends and family

Your most powerful network, contrary to popular belief, is not online with job boards or social platforms. And it's certainly not your peers, who may be in the same predicament you are – looking for quality jobs. No, the best network is composed of the people who actually raised you and those whom they would consider their close personal and professional friends.

These are the people who know you, love you, and most importantly, want to help you succeed. Asking for their help is one of the greatest compliments you can give. It shows you respect them and value their opinions.

If you happen to be disconnected from your parents or the parent/child relationship is not a good one, you still know other adults who can be powerful and influential in building your network. These could include a former high school teacher, a previous summer employer, an athletic coach or other adults who were present in your life during your childhood development.

It's a process

You'll find that many things in professional life follow a process. The job of getting a job is no different. This is the process I strongly recommend you follow, and yes, it may seem laborious at times, but it is effective.

Recordkeeping 101

Begin by creating a document (spreadsheet or word doc in table format) listing every one of your adult relationships; those individuals you believe would be willing to spend 30 minutes with you and provide career advice. Note that I said *provide advice*. I didn't say give you a job. There is a huge distinction between the two.

At a minimum, you'll want to have at least 10 viable contacts to get started. You can certainly include more and are encouraged to do so if possible. The important thing is to identify those adults you have a close personal connection with. Often, moms – those who may have taken time out of the workforce – can be tremendous influencers and connectors. And their networks can be extensive. Don't assume that they need to be actively working either to be of benefit in your networking efforts.

Use the document to identify all the relevant information you can find for your contacts, including work and mobile phone numbers, home and business addresses, email addresses, etc. It's okay if you only start with a single phone number, but you'll want to acquire the other information in time and the sample worksheet I've provided is a good place to start. It's also the best place to make notes on your meetings, keep schedules, track progress and highlight necessary follow-up requirements.

An expanded version of this document will become essential as your network grows to include other professionals. We will have more discussion on that later.

On the following pages is a brief example of a format I've used in the past. Pay particular attention to the comments and examples I provide in the Activity column. This is the type of information capturing and activity that will keep your network alive and your efforts successful.

Contact	Background	Contact
Jan Stevens	Friend of Parents; CFO, Miller Mining	xxx-xxxx (m) xxx-xxxx (o) xxx-xxxx (h) jstevens@ mm.com
Mark Smith	Summer Intern Mgr. Manager, Paramount Café	xxx-xxxx (m) xxx-xxxx (o) xxx-xxxx (h) msmith@pc.com
Bill Robertson	Retired, Former partner Carson Law Firm	xxx-xxxx (m) xxx-xxxx (o) xxx-xxxx (h) bwr39@gmail. com
Your list should have at least 10 names to start!		

Activity
2.24.14: Intro call to Jan. Scheduled mtg. for 2.28.14 at Exeter Donut Shop 9:00am. **2.28.14:** Great meeting! Jan provided two additional contacts: Mary Jacobsen (Mgr. at Voltaire Software) and Steve Parsons (CMO of PKLN Advertising). *Mrs. Stevens will make introductions by late March!*
3.2.14: Intro call to Mark. Scheduled mtg. for 3.5.14 at Mark's house, 10:30 am. **3.5.14:** Mtg. with Mark not overly productive, but he promised to identify another name or two for me to contact. *Follow-up with Mark by March 15.*
3.3.14: Intro call to Bill. Scheduled mtg. for 3.4.14 at Starbucks, Kings Center for 3:00 pm. **3.4.14:** Spent over one hour with Mr. Robertson! He named three companies I should connect with. Asked for soft copy of my resume and he will forward to his contacts. *Follow up with him by April 1 at the latest!*

Getting caffeinated

Now the fun begins. Find your courage and begin calling your network. Don't settle for just one or two contacts. Call everyone on the list. I know from experience there will be a tendency to get comfortable once you've connected with the first few individuals. This is a numbers game, and it requires you to make the calls – all the calls.

The objective is to pack your schedule with as many coffee chats as you can handle. If you attend college away from your home, you may have limited opportunities to meet with these people, so make the most of the time when you are home and schedule multiple meetings.

How do you actually start these conversations? You do it with two simple questions.

The first question: Say exactly this:

Mr., Mrs., . . . I am going to be graduating from college this year and I wondered if you might be able to meet me for coffee? I would love to get your perspective and any advice you could offer as I begin my job search.

Why use this specific language? It's because you have just asked for help from someone who knows you and cares about you. Remember this: They want to help you! And know this: You have not asked them for a job! This makes your request safe, where they have no obligation beyond a half-hour commitment of their time. What you'll hear in response – nine out ten times – is that they would be delighted to meet with you.

**The second question: (After their favorable response),
Say exactly this:**

*Great, is there a convenient time in the next week when we can
get together?*

Why use this specific language? It's because you want to operate
with a sense of urgency; the sooner your contact is able to meet
with you, the better. This isn't because you're desperate. You're
not. It is because you want to get aggressive in your networking
process and you want them to know you're intent on landing a
great job. Book a time to meet! Don't squander the moment.

So remember the comment about art and science? These two
questions are a perfect representation of that. The science resides
in the practice of using this exact language every time, over and
over. The art resides in the specific words chosen. The language is
unassuming, respectful, passionate and timely. Trust me, you will
get your meetings scheduled!

Chapter 4
Game Time

*"It's just a casual conversation with a friend. That's true. But **every** meeting matters. Always come to play."*

Now it's real. We've moved from theory to live conversations. Congratulations. This is about more than simply a conversation, however. There are actually four parts to getting the most out of the face-to-face meetings with your initial network and you need to execute flawlessly on each one of these.

I'll explain each one individually. Much of this may seem obvious to you, but it is remarkable how many individuals I meet who fail to deliver on even one of these, let alone all of them. My advice? Do them all!

Preparation
- **Dress well.** Dress in business casual attire. Yes, you're probably meeting for coffee and it's just with someone you already know, but every meeting is important, and your attire should reflect that.

- **Note ready.** What I'm referring to here is a simple notebook that contains a paper tablet and a sleeve to hold several copies of your resume. Sound old school? Who cares! It speaks business.

- **Clean resume.** One page max. Zero typos. Zero grammatical errors. Be prepared to speak to any aspect of your background. Have several copies in your folio. Don't worry that you have no real experience.

- **Tight story.** Refer to Chapter 1 if necessary. You will probably be asked, "What are you interested in?" or, "What do you want to do?" You'll expedite the conversation if you're completely prepared.

- **Know them.** Yes, you already know your contact, but I mean you should know them *professionally;* their background, business, position, industry, etc. Study up. They'll be pleased and surprised.

- **Prepared questions.** Write down a list of prepared questions but *only* use them in the event the conversation gets off track or stalls. Here are a few examples I recommend:

  - Did you know exactly what you wanted to do when you graduated?

  - How did your career get started?

  - Were there any unusual detours along the way?

  - How has the job market changed for young graduates today?

  - What are qualities you've looked for when hiring?

These six fundamentals of preparation will virtually assure you of a productive meeting. Later in this guide, I'll offer more insight on these essentials, because your meetings with actual decision-makers and influencers will require a slightly different approach.

Discussion

- **Be early.** Nothing says, I'm not serious, more than being late. If you've scheduled your meeting in an unfamiliar place, be certain you know how to get there, how long it will take you and where you can park. Common sense, I know, but leave nothing to chance. And in the ultra-rare event where tragedy strikes and you're not going to be on time, make sure you call your contact and let them know. (Note: How will you contact them if you're going to be delayed? You'll call their mobile number, which you asked for when you scheduled this meeting, and it's listed in your network document!)

- **Get to business.** When your contact arrives, it is acceptable – even desirable – to chat casually for a bit, but be aware you have only a limited amount of time. This means getting down to business. Re-state your appreciation for the meeting and your objective of what you'd like to accomplish – seek their advice and counsel. Again, this establishes a safe platform for your meeting, where they have no obligation beyond providing guidance to you.

- **Enjoy yourself.** These meetings should be fun and comfortable. Relax. Ask if you can take notes. Be astute to those parts of the conversation where you weren't fully prepared for questions they asked. This will help you in future meetings with others. Every experience is cumulative and the more you're interacting with people, the more effective you will become in this process.

- **Listen intently.** After all, you *did* ask them for their insight and advice. You may find the conversation enlightening and informative. In some instances, it may prove less fruitful, but applying your full attention is essential. You never know when an informational nugget may present itself that could prove valuable in your search. Which leads us to the most important aspect of the meeting.

The close

- **Collect names.** Be especially attuned during your conversation to any suggestions your contact has about potential companies or individuals they believe would be a good match for you. Act like a reporter. Ask follow-up questions including:

  - How have you worked with them in the past?

  - Is this a person (or company) you could introduce me to?

  - Do you know if they're looking to add staff?

Any or all of these questions can create the opportunity to meet another new contact. And now comes the most critical part of your entire conversation and it will occur as you're wrapping up. If you haven't yet discovered any new potential contacts, ask this question, and yes, ask it in exactly this manner:

Are there one or two other individuals you believe I may benefit from having a conversation with?

This seems fairly innocuous, but it's incredibly powerful. In essence, you are asking for their permission to contact other influential people they know. Their answer will lead you in one of two directions:

1. If they have suggestions right then, gather the information you need. Ask if they would prefer to make the introduction(s), or if you should make the contact(s) on your own. If the latter, be sure you get their name with correct spelling, the name of their company, and a sense

of timing when you can begin making contact. In many cases, your friend may want to make an initial call to notify the individual you will be calling.

2. If they don't have immediate suggestions for you, ask your friend if they wouldn't mind giving this some thought,where you can follow-up (within a week) and revisit your request.

The vital thing to remember here is: do not leave this meeting without either collecting the names of one or two potential new contacts, or at least asking your friend for permission to call them again soon for their suggestions on additional contacts.

Why is this so important? It's because every meeting is an opportunity for you to expand your network. It's also important because you are accessing *their* professional network and these are trusted relationships developed over a lifetime. In other words, these contacts are pure gold! These people are often managers, business owners and leaders who can influence hiring decisions within their organizations.

Follow-up

- **End promptly.** If you asked for 30 minutes of their time, be sure you end the meeting at 30 minutes. If they want to continue, then certainly you should accommodate. In fact, your best meetings will likely run longer than the time you've requested. But you should be the timekeeper and respectful of their schedule.

- **Thank them.** As you wrap up, be sure to thank them for meeting with you. You don't need to gush. However, expressing your sincere appreciation confirms to them that their time was well spent and is appreciated.

- **Write them.** There are few things as powerful as a hand-written thank-you message. Remember, you have been meeting with an individual who is likely 50 years old (or older) and their generation still values the courtesy of a personalized note. So write them immediately and see that your note gets in their hands within the next few days. Know this: Emails and text messages are quickly discarded; hand written thank-you cards rarely are.

- **Call them.** Maintain the relationship by calling them occasionally. They will be interested in how you're progressing. And they'll certainly be interested in how your meetings went with the contacts they provided you. Let them know. Keep them informed. Don't be shy about asking for additional advice. They will by joyful and pleased when you secure your first position, especially if they had a hand in the process.

Chapter 5

Your Second Level Network

*"The effort you apply towards research is a direct reflection of **how serious you are** about winning a position."*

When you diligently follow the process discussed in the previous chapter, you likely will find your schedule very full. After all, just apply the simple math. If you start by meeting with 10 friends and each refers you to one or two other individuals, you will soon find you have the opportunity to meet with up to 30 professionals. Think social platforms will provide that same opportunity? Not a chance.

This second level of your network is extremely important and will mostly consist of people I call influencers. These are the individuals who can either influence hiring decisions or connect you with those who can. And the stakes are higher with these folks. You may only get one shot with them, so your presence, story, interviewing skills and follow-up all need to be impeccable. Don't panic; your initial network meetings have helped prepare you for this.

Research on steroids

There is one thing that will always delight when you're meeting with influencers, and that's the extensive amount of research you'll do in preparation. I'm not talking about just visiting the company's website so that you have a cursory knowledge of the organization. Rather, I'm referring to the deep study required to know the firm, their industry, competitive position, challenges and opportunities for growth – of which you'd like to be a part!

There is no shortcut here. Spend time online. Download white papers. Read news articles and annual reports so that your understanding is functional and accurate. Influencers can sniff out phoniness in a heartbeat. If they ask what you know about their company – and most influencers will – you can't bluff, and only a knowledge that comes from deep research will equip you to have a quality conversation.

You would be stunned to know how many individuals I've interviewed who know nothing about me, my role, my department, my company or my industry. What's my natural impression of them? They're apathetic. I don't know of many companies that look for apathy when hiring a new associate.

So, yes, spend the time; go deep, read incessantly; uncover things that others won't. This is hard, intensive work, but it's the easiest route to separating yourself from the pack.

Quite simply, influencers will be left with a single, memorable impression: You cared enough to know them *before* you came in. That single impression alone can win you a position.

Applying your knowledge

How you apply that knowledge in conversation with an influencer is a delicate matter. Yes, you'll be eager to discuss what you've learned through your research, especially if you're asked, but you should never use this knowledge to impress. Instead, think if it as a tool to be used conversationally during the normal course of an interview. It's not difficult to find these opportunities. The important thing is to let these moments happen naturally.

Record keeping 201

Earlier, I provided an example of a document that allows you to manage important information on your first level of contacts. Effectively managing your second level network requires the same measure of diligence, but much more detail.

My intention is not to lose you in a maze of project management, so the following example I've provided is simply a reference tool. But, like most individuals, you have now assembled a pile of papers including notes, contacts, phone numbers, action items and research, that is increasingly becoming a source of anxiety. This second level network document is a single location that will help bring order to chaos.

Notice the degree of detail provided in the Activity and Research columns. You'll want and need to keep this same type of extensive record, because your second level network will grow rapidly and you'll need to maintain an accurate account of meetings, schedules, follow-up activity and most importantly, the research you've conducted on each individual and company. Trust me, you'll need this.

Company	Contacts
Voltaire Software (referred by Jan Stevens)	**Mary Jacobsen** SVP, Business Development xxx-xxxx (m) xxx-xxxx (o) **Carter Douglas** Director, Customer Relations xxx-xxxx (m) xxx-xxxx (o) **Pat Andrews** HR Manager xxx-xxxx (m) xxx-xxxx (o)
PKLN Advertising (referred by Jan Stevens)	Steve Parsons COO xxx-xxxx (m) xxx-xxxx (o) Ann Girard Creative Director xxx-xxxx (m) xxx-xxxx (o)
Evans Metals (referred by Amy Girard)	Karen Sheehan VP Operations xxx-xxxx (m) xxx-xxxx (o)

Activity	Research
3.25.14: Jan Stevens called Mary to make soft introduction and let her know I'd be calling. **3.25.14:** Called Mary to schedule a meeting **4.6.14:** Had 1st meeting with Mary; Sent thank you note and scheduled Follow-up meeting with her Director, Carter Douglas. **4.15.14:** Met with Carter. Discussed entry-level position in customer care. He sent my resume to Pat in HR. **5.4.14:** Received call from Pat Andrews and had a phone interview. I was prepared and think it went well!	**Voltaire Software;** founded in 1996 by three partners who worked at a global cm firm previously. Focus is project management software for cm firms. They recently acquired a rival firm and doubled their sales in 2013. Rapidly growing in fiercely competitive space. **Mary Jacobson** is SVP of Bus. Dev. 30 years of experience and has been with Voltaire since the beginning. Knows Jan from college; same sorority. I went to HS with her oldest daughter, Megan. Smart person! **Carter Douglas** is Director of customer relations and a great guy; could see myself working for him! **Pat Andrews** is HR manager. New to Voltaire and came from recently acquired company. A bit stiff and difficult to get close to, but I think Carter is an advocate for me.
3.25.14: Jan Stevens called Steve and paved meeting for time mid April. Call Steve 4.15. **4.15.14:** Called Steve. Scheduled meeting in their downtown office for 9:00, 4.18. Sent soft copy of my resume at his request. **4.18.14:** Met with Steve and Ann Girard. Talked for an hour, which I thought was good sign. No current openings but Ann suggested I contact her friend, Karen Sheehan, who works at Evans Metals. They're neighbors and Ann says they're hiring. **4.22.14**: Called Karen at Evans Metals and scheduled meeting.	**PKLN** is a regional ad agency specializing in travel and commercial business. The firm is 30+ years old. Recent focus on digital media as a specialty and it's the largest growth area of their business. Competitors include XXX, XXX and XXX. **Steve Parson** is an advertising veteran. Started in one of Chicago's largest firms; moved to NY for 5-year stint and then formed PKLN with three partners in 1980. Has won numerous industry awards and serves on board of directors of two local charities, one of which Jan Stevens is on as well. He is a partner in PKLN and COO. **Ann Girard** is the Creative Director for PKLN. I loved her! Great enthusiasm, really quick-witted, and very engaging in conversation. Ann is married with two young kids; they love to ski.
4.22.14: Called Karen Sheehan at the suggestion of Ann Girard (PKLN Advertising). Scheduled meeting at their office for 5/3. **5.3.14:** Meeting pending . . .	**Evans Metals** is a parts manufacturer for the aerospace industry. They have manufacturing facilities in Birmingham, AL and San Diego, CA. If was difficult to find detailed information on Evans, because much of their work is focused on the defense industry (top secret), but they've been in business for 22 years and have over 160 employees. The company is privately held. **Karen Sheen** is the operations VP. Online research revealed she earned her MBA from SDSU in 2006, so she has obviously fast-tracked her career.

Really?

Okay, one review of this spreadsheet and I already know the question you're asking. Is all this really necessary? Yes, it is. I'm asking you to provide this granular level of information in your record keeping not to make your life more difficult, but rather to make your opportunities more profound.

Chapter 6
Hidden Benefits

"Savor the full experience in the job of getting a job. It will pay dividends for your entire life."

Simply scheduling this increasing activity will be challenging. Add the necessary research and preparation required for each meeting, and the process can seem daunting. Do not get overwhelmed. In fact, now is a good time to reflect on the hidden benefits of this process.

The joy of pure discovery
Humor me here. I have a confession to make: I love work! Okay, that may sound a little nutty, and there have certainly been phases of my career where redundant tasks have been prevalent and inspired moments few. But overall, my career has exposed me to fascinating businesses and industries and a wealth of engaging and interesting people. All of this has contributed to the richness of my professional life.

If you embrace the job of getting a job with a student's heart, you are likely to learn more about American enterprise than you could have ever imagined. The world of business is incredibly diverse and there are companies and industries hiring talented individuals that you've never considered.

As your network grows – and you're conducting the required research in preparation for your growing schedule of meetings – think of this as a lesson in discovery. You may have earned a degree in computer science with the hope of one day working for Google, only to discover that this foundational scholastic knowledge can be applied at a mid-stream energy company building infrastructure to carry newly discovered natural gas from a shale-gas play in western Pennsylvania. Who knew? And this discovery may occur from simple research you conducted in preparation for one of your network meetings.

It's a big world. Read, research and learn as part of your journey. It will open up new paths of opportunity for you, and quite honestly, it will make you more conversationally interesting with your professional contacts.

The secret passage

Your research will not only uncover new business opportunities you weren't previously aware of, you'll find that the connections within your network will begin to link together. For example, you may discover that one of your contacts who works in a law firm, lives in the same neighborhood as one of your initial friends and family relationships.

Surprisingly, they both serve on the board of directors for a financial services company. So what? Well, it just happens that one of your other contacts you met with previously, suggested you meet with Steve, who is the sales manager of the same financial services firm. Bingo. Now you have interrelated contacts that significantly increase your chances of getting in front of the right people.

If this sounds unlikely, it's not. I've seen this play out hundreds of times in my career. The broader your network becomes, the more opportunities of secret passage you'll encounter.

The gift that keeps on giving

Since you're applying so much effort in building a meaningful network, there may be a tendency to forget about it once you've secured your first job. Don't let that happen. In all likelihood, you will work for many different firms throughout your career, and your network will prove invaluable in helping you maintain a progressive path where you're growing professionally and financially.

Chapter 7
Tournament Time

"All your work up to this point was designed to get you in front of influencers. Now that you're there, do all of these things and do them exceptionally well."

It would be a mistake to imply that the job of getting a job is a linear process. In other words, events in your search for a job won't always progress in a logical order, and your networking discussions may take many different turns. In fact, the coffee chats you started with friends and family and expanded to include the next layer of contacts, should all be considered part of the interviewing process.

If you're fortunate, you may not need to move beyond your initial networking group to land a great starting position. So the lesson here is, you are always being watched and closely evaluated, even just when meeting with an individual for advice and information gathering.

If, however, you're operating heavily in your second level network, then you'll want to ratchet up your intensity. This is the land where influencers play, and it's certainly the arena where the best positions will be revealed to the best candidates. If the work and effort you applied with initial network contacts was considered game time, think of your discussions with second level network contacts as tournament time. It's even more important now.

Which brings me to another piece of advice I can offer. It's about presence. I wish I could claim it for my own, but I learned it earlier in my career from my good friend Robert, who in many respects served as a brief and important mentor to me. He at one time headed up corporate communications for Coors Brewing Co., and later became a partner in a pioneering cable television company.

Presence

Somewhere, mid-career, I was considering an industry change, which I've done multiple times. I turned to Robert for advice and he gave me plenty. But, one thing in particular he said highlighted the absolute importance of standing out with influencers. He described it as presence and explained that it is essential when meeting with influencers they know that you're necessary, present and available.

In his words, he described this as a mindset of **me–here–now**. What he was really saying is that one simply doesn't know when opportunity may occur, and it's imperative that every meeting with every individual is approached from the standpoint of conveying that you are valuable, you're ready and you can help the organization immediately.

Owning this perspective is certainly no guarantee that job offers will flow from every conversation, but you never know when a company will have need. And by adopting this simple philosophy you leave a lasting impression with the individual you're meeting with. That's important, because whether they have a need at that moment or sometime in the future, they are far more likely to remember you.

I've personally experienced how this same philosophy can pay dividends as one's career evolves. Many times, I've seen organizations uncover new opportunities or identify problems that require an individual owner. By simply raising my hand, and being assertive with a me-here-now attitude, I've witnessed my own career path accelerate into new and unforeseen areas. Believe me, it works.

Every meeting now is a real interview

Consider every meeting you have with a second level network influencer a real interview. Granted, they may not have current open positions posted. They may simply be meeting with you as a favor to one of your first level network friends. But, these are *influencers*; professionals who can make something happen for you. That *something* might be within their organization or with an important connection to another professional relationship.

In a previous chapter, I discussed the four parts of a successful meeting. With your second level network contacts – influencers, some of the same principles apply, but there are also subtle and important differences. Here, I'll discuss three of those four elements – preparation, discussion, follow up – as these are cornerstones of effective meetings with influencers. As I mentioned earlier, do all of these!

Preparation
- **Dress well.** Dress in business attire. For men, that means wearing a suit and tie. If you don't have nice dress shoes, buy a pair. And for God's sake, wear socks! For women, business dress applies.

- **Note ready.** Remember, you will be taking notes, and you'll already have a list of prepared questions.

- **Clean resume.** Include all work related experience, even summer jobs. Internships are meaningful. Be prepared to speak to every aspect of your resume. Don't embellish.

- **Tight story.** The original story you've developed should serve you well, but depending on the influencer you're meeting with, your story may be modified slightly to better fit the discussion.

- **Know them.** This is what all your hard research has been about. Know everything possible about your influencer, their company and their industry. Use your knowledge conversationally; don't force.

- **Prepared questions.** Generally, you will be asked at the end of a discussion if you have any questions. Don't miss the opportunity. The type of questions you ask, says a lot to the influencer about who you are. Here are a few examples to give you a flavor of questions that will resonate well:

  - I noticed when doing some homework that your firm has grown recently through acquisition. Is that a defined strategy or is it that you're just finding good opportunities in this environment?

  - What do you see as your greatest challenges and opportunities in the next three years?

  - Are there any particular areas of your organization where you're looking to add or upgrade talent in the next few months?

  - I see that you joined the company six years ago. Were you looking for a new challenge, or how did that come about?

- What do you view as the greatest threat to your industry in the near future? How is your firm positioned or preparing to deal with that?

Obviously, you will tailor your own questions based upon your research and what you discover about the influencer and their company. The point is, ask probing questions that require more than a yes or no answer. There is a reason for this:

When they're talking, you're winning

Another golden nugget of advice my friend Robert provided is the idea that an interview is a discussion that you have a measure of control over. Interesting. Most candidates approach a meeting or interview with trepidation and anxiety. That needn't be. Your advantage – and it's a big one – is that you're prepared. You know a lot more about the person interviewing you and their company than they know about you. Use this to your benefit.

How? By asking those timely and thoughtful questions throughout your discussion. It seems counterintuitive. You are there so they can learn about you. But make no mistake, whether you are doing the talking or they are, you are always being watched. They are watching your body language. Are you listening? Do you appear interested? Are you taking notes? Are you focused on them?

This is why my friend says, "when they're talking . . . you're winning." People generally like to talk about themselves, so take the offensive, ask some good open-ended questions and get them talking! For sure, the interview is still occurring, but now it's more on your terms, not just theirs.

Discussion

- **Be early.** I suggest arriving 5-10 minutes early for your meeting. Any more than that, and you could be inconveniencing their schedule. Arriving late is never ever acceptable. Those that show up late are toast before the meeting even begins.

  As you're waiting to meet your influencer, take a few deep breaths. This will help calm you, and also give you a moment to reflect on how well prepared you are for this meeting. Remember, you've done your homework, and this person is seeing you upon the request of a friend from your initial network. You have a huge advantage over other candidates who won't have this same warm introduction.

- **First impressions.** This is going to sound like a parent, which I am, but I'm going state the obvious anyway. Remember, in most cases, the influencer you're meeting with is generally someone seasoned in business with years of experience. In other words they're older than you, probably by many years. Older professionals are due certain respects that include:

  - **A firm handshake;** doesn't matter whether you are male or female. A firm handshake signals confidence.

  - **Eye contact;** looking them squarely in the eye indicates you're engaged and attentive.

  - **Surname;** address your influencer by Mr. Ms. Mrs. Let them tell *you* if they prefer you use their first name. Don't assume.

  - **Your appreciation;** smile and let them know how thankful you are to have this meeting.

Recognize that opinions are generally formed in the first two minutes, good and bad. These things are just basic table stakes that earn you entry into the next part of your important conversation. Again, you'd be shocked to discover how many candidates fail in the first minute.

- **Show Time.** The actual discussion is what you've been waiting for! You are meeting with an influencer who can affect your career. So be poised and apply your A-game. And while the personality you bring to the conversation is uniquely your own, there are a few fundamentals you must exhibit:

  - **Enthusiasm;** don't effuse excessively, but the energy you apply to this discussion is important and will be clearly evident.

  - **Listening;** a good listener never interrupts; a good listener answers accurately; a good listener knows when to ask questions.

  - **Sincerity;** I have mentioned this before: be authentic and honest. Don't bluff.

  - **Me, Here, Now;** Discussed previously, exude the confidence that lets them know you're equipped, ready and available.

- **Buying Signals.** Twenty minutes into the discussion, you'll have a good sense on how things are progressing. Remember, people hire people they'd like to work with. If the chemistry is not happening, don't force it. Not every interview is going to end in a job offer. On the other hand, if you're feeling positive about your conversation, chances are your influencer is as well. So you need to be aware of subtle buying signals; indications of interest in you. These are a few examples and they'll typically come in the form of a question, like:

- Do you have time to stay a bit longer? I'd like you to meet one of my associates. *Your answer: Absolutely.*

- How soon would you be available to start? *Your answer: Immediately, although I would like to be respectful of my current employer (if you're already working) and provide them two-week notice.*

- You mentioned you're looking for a position in [finance, marketing, etc.], but would you be open to another role in [sales support, business development, etc.]? *Your answer: Certainly. What I'm really looking for is an opportunity to start my career with a great company, and I'm open to considering any role where you have an immediate need.*

- Are you willing to relocate? *Your answer: Absolutely.*

- Would you be available to come back tomorrow and meet a few other members of the team? *Your answer: Absolutely.*

Of course, there may be other signals, but the important thing is to recognize when they're occurring and to be able to respond definitively and with conviction.

- **Ask for the order.** Every influencer you meet will be uniquely different. Some may be reserved and guarded; others more gregarious and conversational. Yet they all will generally exhibit a few common characteristics. They're about business and they're direct. Subsequently, you should be also. If you believe your discussion has gone well, it's perfectly acceptable, even expected, for you to ask a few direct questions as the meeting is wrapping up. For example:

  - Do you anticipate any opportunities within your organization where I might be a good fit?

  - How quickly are you looking to fill those positions?

- Are there any other associates in your company you believe it would be beneficial for me to meet with?

- Do you have everything you need from me or is there anything else I can provide? References?

• **The Compensation Question.** Invariably when you're discussing a specific role, you'll be asked – in one form or another – what your salary requirements are. Expect this and be ready to answer with a dollar amount. It's annoying to an influencer when a candidate is evasive, or even worse, answers the question by asking how much the position pays. So, you will want to have done your homework on compensation for similar roles. I've found this approach to be effective:

I believe an annual compensation package of [$45,000, $55,000, $65,000, etc.] is reasonable for the qualities I will bring to your organization. Of course, I recognize this is an entry-level position, and I'm flexible on starting salary, as long as I have the opportunity to prove my value and to advance within the organization.

• **Wrap-up.** These may appear to be housekeeping items, but they matter:

- **Finish on schedule**. Don't extend the conversation beyond your allotted time, unless your influencer wants to.

- **Say thanks**. A simple and sincere thank you for the opportunity to meet with them.

- **Get their information.** Ask your influencer for a business card. It has important contact information you'll need.

- **Next steps.** Confirm any action items or follow-up requested of you in your discussion and confirm dates for when any activity is expected.

Follow-up

- **The power of a handwritten note:** I know, I talked about this in an earlier chapter, but it's worth repeating. After your interview follow up promptly and do it properly. In some cases, an interview may include meetings with several individuals. If that's the case, follow up with everyone who was present. Here's how:

  - The message should be personalized in a handwritten thank-you note

  - The message should capture elements of your conversation you were particularly excited about

  - The message should be sincere, positive and reflect your appreciation for the time they offered you

  - The message should also express how interested you are in becoming a part of their organization

What about email? Is email a suitable method of thanking your influencer for meeting with you? Perhaps, but it's not nearly as effective as the handwritten note. Email is better suited for subsequent contact and for checking in with these individuals at frequent intervals so that you remain top of mind.

To the ends of the earth

A good friend told me a story recently about an individual who had interviewed for a wholesaling position within our company. This was an extremely desirable role in the financial services industry and the competition was fierce. Upon completing his interview with the hiring manager, the candidate wrote a personal note as follow-up, expressing his appreciation for being considered.

That night, the hiring manager was traveling to another city and the candidate was astute enough to ask where he would be staying. The candidate then had his note sent via overnight early-morning delivery to the destination hotel where the hiring manager was staying.

After opening the overnight package (and personal note) the next morning, the surprised manager called the candidate and hired him. When asked why he was selected, the manager said, "Because any professional who is *that* attentive to the importance of timely follow-up, is the type of professional I want working for me."

Promptness can make all the difference.

Chapter 8
The Offer

*"It's not just about the money. Your first **meaningful** job is about so much more."*

Few things professionally can be as electrifying as being offered a new position. At a very fundamental level, an offer says you are wanted and needed; things most human beings treasure as affirmation that they matter. Yet few things hinder your rational thinking more than an offer. Why? It's because you are operating in an emotional state of exhilaration, which can skew your abilities to evaluate an offer analytically.

Is the position right for you?
Don't get me wrong. You should be thrilled, and it's proper to let the person extending the offer know that you are. But the offered position should also be one that meets the definition of your first *meaningful* job. What exactly do I mean by that?

In my experience, I've seen many college graduates seeking permanent work focus on the elements of an offer that may seem important at the time – starting salary, commute time, benefits, paid days off, etc. – but ultimately prove to be of little value in accelerating a young career. That's why you should consider these questions (and others) upon receiving your offer:

1. Does the position provide opportunity for rapid learning and professional growth?

2. Do you believe your new manager will be an effective teacher and coach?

3. Do you see your fellow associates as being supportive, helpful and collaborative?

4. Is the environment competitive (not necessarily a bad thing), and how will you integrate yourself?

5. Is the company financially sound? How do you know?

6. Is the industry – in which the company operates – interesting to you?

7. Does the company have a long-term strategic plan and vision?

8. Do the associates believe in this plan?

9. Could you be required to relocate at some point and are you prepared to do that?

10. Have other young associates progressed quickly in either new positions or with new responsibilities?

Much like the earlier effort of defining your personal story, I'm encouraging you to work through a similar mental exercise to determine if this offer aligns with your natural gifts. And the reason is simple. When you find a position that affords you the ability to apply your best qualities in a professional work environment, then the experience will be meaningful. That's it.

So be deliberate and make an informed, wise decision. Am I suggesting you decline this opportunity that you worked exceptionally hard to earn? No, and in fact you and the offering firm wouldn't even be at this stage without you both having a high level of confidence that the match is right. I am suggesting, however, that you ask yourself if you're accepting this role for the right reasons.

Salary negotiation

I have mixed feelings about this one, so recognize I'm just offering my opinion. There isn't necessarily a right or wrong approach to salary negotiation. Upon receiving a verbal offer, the offering manager will typically identify the position, desired start date and compensation package. You may want to consider a counter-offer where you request a higher level of compensation.

This is delicate. At a time when there are tens of thousands of talented college graduates looking for quality jobs, a counter-offer can be perceived by the hiring manager that you are unappreciative. That can leave a sour taste. On the other hand, many managers anticipate that candidates will counter the initial offer, and by failing to do so, you may leave dollars on the table.

Personally, I appreciate the individual who has asked for an appropriate level of compensation during the interview process, and doesn't attempt to negotiate for something more once an offer has been extended. But as mentioned, this is a personal bias and not necessarily a reflection of how you should manage your own situation. Yes, money is important, but it's only one element of this new position. Ask yourself this question: Does this offer reflect fair compensation for this early stage in my career? If you can answer affirmatively, accept the offer. If you can't, you may want to negotiate.

Chapter 9

Congratulations, you've won! Now what?

"You know that expression about 'never getting a second chance to make a good first impression?' Well, it's somewhat true. So make your first impression count!"

The first 90 days.

You've won the position. Congratulations! With winning, however, there are accompanying expectations. You've earned this new role based upon the qualities your hiring manager believes you will apply to your work, and the value they expect you to bring to the company. Don't disappoint. That's why the first 90 days in your new position will not only confirm their wise decision of hiring you, but these three months will largely define your personal brand for those throughout the organization.

What gets noticed?

There are a few universal qualities that every company appreciates from a newly hired associate. Notice I said company and not peers. Certain peers may be wary about your intentions as you strive to over-deliver. Why? That's because you were hired to be an asset to the company, but to current associates, you may be perceived as a threat. My response is, "who cares!" Working environments are inherently competitive. So win the attention and favor of key influencers in the firm, and do it by applying these practices:

1. **Work harder than others.** This means showing up early and going home a bit later that expected; even avoiding the full hour-long lunches afforded many associates. (Note: In some cases, you may have a position that is defined by the Fair Labor Standards Act (FLSA) as non-exempt, which means you are compensated on an hourly basis. Depending upon company policy, this may require that you work only a scheduled 40-hour week). But, if your role is considered exempt, you have the freedom to apply extra time and effort. Do it, and do it consistently. *Influencers will see this additional effort.*

2. **Ask questions;** a lot of questions. Everyone recognizes you are new. You probably know little about your position, the company and the industry you now operate in. So one of the best ways to learn quickly is to find those around you willing to educate and help. Lean on them and always remind them how much you appreciate their support. Can incessant questions become annoying? Perhaps, so work through the things you're expected to learn independently and save your questions for the complex issues that only seasoned associates know. *Influencers will appreciate your thirst to learn.*

3. **Self-study.** Yes, you want and need a reasonable work-life balance, but find the time after hours or on weekends to read everything you can to accelerate your understanding in this new venture. Thank goodness Al Gore created the Internet (search for this on YouTube!) because all the information you'll need is available at your fingertips on your mobile device. Read about your industry. Study your competitors. Identify what you believe they're doing well and not. Look at macro issues like policy and the economy to discover other external influences your company may need to contend with. The point is, take control of your own education. You will have ample opportunities to offer insight and suggestions. *Influencers will notice your expanding knowledge.*

4. **Raise your hand.** Many companies are operating very lean today, which is something you've probably discovered in your job search. Because of that, managers need reliable associates they can ask to take on new or additional assignments. Be one of those associates. Even if the request is for a project you don't feel fully equipped to assist on, take it on anyway. *Influencers will recognize your commitment.*

So what's the point of all this? Are you just trying to impress the boss at the risk of alienating your co-workers? No. You're establishing work habits that will become part of your professional DNA. I can tell you, with very few exceptions, those individuals who start their career exhibiting these qualities are likely to be those who see their careers advance more rapidly than others. And interestingly, these work characteristics become living examples that managers encourage other associates to emulate. Do these consistently and your professional adventure will be off to a remarkable start.

Epilogue

Personal Stories of Pain and Joy

> *"I wouldn't have missed a single minute of it. Not for the whole world"* – from Hearts in Atlantis, Stephen King"

I want to thank you for a few things. First, I appreciate you purchasing this book, although my own monetary reward had little if anything to do with the reason I wrote this. Thank you, anyway, though, and I hope you find value in your investment. Secondly, thanks for enduring what at times must have seemed like an opinionated and humorless discussion. That wasn't the intention. I can assure you, the writing of this book was truly a joyful experience for me and hopefully, among the pages, you can glimpse a measure of my passion for helping young professionals.

Over the course of a very fulfilling professional career, I've had more encounters with newly hired associates than I can recall. Some of these interactions have been painful to witness, while others have been quite inspirational. I wanted to include a few examples. Names have obviously been changed to protect identities.

Ultimately, the experiences in our lives become the nuclei of stories. And in stories, we're offered the gift of learning.

How you write says a lot about who you are
One time a co-worker forwarded a resume and cover letter from a highly recommended college graduate, and asked me if we were hiring in our marketing department. Many managers, even if not actively hiring, are always looking for talented candidates. I'm very much like this. I like to build a bench.

When I began reading this individual's cover letter, I only reached the second sentence before realizing I was in for a grammatical hot mess. Opportunity over. If you don't care enough to proof and re-proof your letter of introduction and your resume, why would I believe you'll care about the business I'm looking to hire you into?

Proofing only takes a few minutes. And never, ever rely solely on spell-check to find mistakes. Ask others to proof if necessary.

Sometimes a great notion

I had the pleasure last year of meeting with a college graduate seeking simple advice. This occurred upon the prompting of his parents. He and I had a great discussion and I hit the typical highlights of "do this" and "don't do this" during the job-seeking process.

This young man worked at youth camp overseas during the summer following his graduation and the next I heard from him, he had returned to the states and had won a position at a small energy company in southern California. Actually, I didn't hear directly from him, but I heard from his parents. And this is what he asked them to tell me:

"Tell Mr. Mathies that his advice on doing the hard but necessary research on a company before my interview is what got me this job. I have no doubt about it. In fact when I interviewed, I knew more about the company, its history and its clients than the son of the founder, who conducted the interview! Among an army of candidates interviewing for the position, I won! Tell Mike, he was right."

These are gratifying and confirming moments for me.

Little things that hurt, and then . . .

Last year, I provided counsel to a young women looking for a quality position in a certain field. We covered many of the fundamentals discussed in this guide. When we met a few months later she had built her initial network and one particular meeting expanded into a second-level network interview with a senior vice president at a very prominent technology company. She thought she had performed extremely well in the interview and sensed several buying signals.

Then she waited. And waited. She followed up with her contact and with the HR manager, yet received no indication on their hiring decision. When she finally got a call from the HR manager informing her that she had not been selected for the open position, it was explained that she didn't have industry experience; a valid comment and something entirely out her control.

And then, as a parting shot, the manager told her she had a typo on her cover letter. Already disappointed at hearing the news she'd not been selected, she now had to endure what seemed like an unnecessary criticism. Yes, these were hard words to hear, but important. Remember what we discussed earlier? Zero typos. Zero grammatical errors.

Postscript: A few month's later, the young woman received a call from the same HR manager alerting her that a new position, not yet posted, would be opening and they would like her to come in and interview for it. Two weeks later, this young woman had won the position. In hindsight, the 'scolding' the HR manager had provided about the cover letter typo after the first interview, was in fact 'advice' that would help her not make that mistake again, and ultimately secure the next opportunity they had.

What a difference a tie makes

A friend and colleague told me a story about when he was selected to become an external sales representative for our organization. At the time, a divisional sales manager had asked to meet with five internal desk managers to discuss strategies for the upcoming year. One of the internal managers was my friend. He showed up at the meeting wearing a suit and tie, whereas his fellow associates were dressed in traditional business casual. The meeting was productive and my friend thought that was the end of it.

Two weeks, later, he received a call from the divisional manager asking if he would like to accept a position in field sales – a significant increase in salary and a role internal managers hunger for. He jumped at the opportunity, but he also asked the divisional manager why he was selected amongst his peers. The answer was short and quite direct: "Because you were the only one who dressed professionally for our meeting, and that's the type of individual I want representing us in the field." Who knew?

Small details can often lead to large opportunities.

Just you wait!

I've had the privilege of working with some true HR professionals throughout my career. On the other hand, I've worked with some that should never be allowed to represent a company, let alone influence hiring decisions. One of my daughters tells a favorite story in which she was shredded in an interview with an HR manager:

"An HR manager scheduled a meeting with me after my resume had been kicked over from a 1st level network contact. There wasn't even an actual position, but this person must have felt pressured to see me. Not a good start. From my background profile I completed for the

firm, the manager proceeded to highlight fact that I'd receive an
MIP (minor in possession of alcohol) when I was in college. And
he explained how that poor decision would likely have a negative
influence on my entire professional career. Ouch!"

"What I found most interesting, and aggravating, was that this
manager was scolding me as a parent might reprimand a child
and he was telling me how I should behave. I also learned in the
interview that the manager had two young daughters of his own,
and he implied that they would not make similar mistakes as I did
when they got older. Oh yeah? Just you wait, pal!"

Poor follow-up can be costly
In another instance, a friend asked if I would be willing to
meet with their daughter (we'll call her Ashley), a recent
college graduate, and offer guidance on how to start the process
of finding a job. I seized the opportunity and suggested they have
her call me. Three weeks later (yes, three weeks!), I received a
call from Ashley. Already I'm beginning to question her sense of
urgency and commitment.

We scheduled a meeting at a local coffee shop and for an hour,
I shared my ideas on actionable steps she could take to start the
process; everything from "refining her story," to "networking" to
"interviewing." Ashley had not brought anything to write on, so I
made notes for her. The meeting was pleasant, and I left feeling that
she was energized and ready to get after it. I suggested as next steps
that she send me her resume and call me within a week so we could
review her personal story; something we would continue to refine.

I never heard from her after that meeting. Unfortunately for
Ashley, I had two positions open in my own organization shortly
after we met. I filled those positions with other candidates, even
though Ashley's background and skills would have proven to be
an excellent fit. So instead of securing a position with the first

person she networked with, I hired two other individuals, each at a starting salary of $55,000. What a shame. Energy, attitude, promptness, follow-up; all these things we've discussed are essential.

You just need a start

Two quick stories here, both involving college graduates who reached out to me several years ago at the request of their parents. (Little did they know, they we're actually practicing the first and second level networking model).

Randy had great engagement and conversation skills and I liked him immediately. Recently graduated from college, he didn't know what type of career he wanted to pursue, but he wanted to get to work. I felt his energy and warm personality would be well applied in a sales position, so I asked our desk manager to hire him.

Understand that internal sales can be tedious and demanding work. You're basically making cold calls all day, every day. Randy quickly became a top sales associate and was soon being groomed for an external sales position. During his first year at the company, I had a mentor-type relationship with Randy, sharing many of the sales experiences I'd learned personally and painfully over the years.

Today, Randy is one of the top performing sales associates in his company, and one of the most highly compensated in his industry – earning well over $1 million/year. Not bad for a person not yet 30 years old. All he needed was a start.

Leslie contacted me as a second level influencer, when she was looking to make an early career change. She was personable, organized, enthusiastic and coachable. I had an opening for an events manager at the time and I hired her. She performed exceptionally well in this role while I was at the firm.

Over the next several years, I watched her career progress as her network expanded and ultimately she became one of the top event planners working for firms covering the Olympics and the World Cup.

All she needed was a start.

All *you* need is a start. And now you're equipped. Go get it!

The End

50986059R00038

Made in the USA
Lexington, KY
07 April 2016